The Facts on Famous Artifacts

HOW DID THE PARTHENON GET TO THE BRITISH MUSEUM?

Dwayne Hicks

CREATED BY
Humans

Published in 2027 by The Rosen Publishing Group, Inc.
2544 Clinton Street, Buffalo, NY 14224

First Edition

Editor: Greg Roza
Designer: Michael Flynn

Photo Credits: Cover William Silver/Shutterstock.com; (series background) Yuliya Chsherbakova/Shutterstock.com; p. 5 Lucky-photographer/Shutterstock.com; p. 6 delcarmat/Shutterstock.com; p. 7 Kirk Fisher/Shutterstock.com; p. 8 https://commons.wikimedia.org/wiki/File:Akropolis_by_Leo_von_Klenze.jpg; p. 9 https://commons.wikimedia.org/wiki/File:Map_The_Acropolis_of_Athens_and_its_slopes_1928-1940_-_Touring_Club_Italiano_CART-TRC-37.jpg; p. 11 https://commons.wikimedia.org/wiki/File:Athens_Acropolis_museum_dedication_trireme.jpg; p. 12 Vectorbum/Shutterstock.com; p. 13 tilialucida/Shutterstock.com; p. 14 Leon Rafael/Shutterstock.com; p. 15 nito/Shutterstock.com; p. 17 https://commons.wikimedia.org/wiki/File:Discurso_funebre_pericles.PNG; p. 19 Marcin Niemiec/Shutterstock.com; p. 21 https://commons.wikimedia.org/wiki/File:Venetian_siege_of_Acropolis.jpg; p. 23 https://commons.wikimedia.org/wiki/File:7th_Earl_of_Elgin_by_Anton_Graff_around_1788.jpg; p. 24 gowithstock/Shutterstock.com; p. 25 John Wreford/Shutterstock.com; p. 27 staka99/Shutterstock.com.

Cataloging-in-Publication Data

Names: Hicks, Dwayne.
Title: How did the Parthenon get to the British Museum? / Dwayne Hicks.
Description: Buffalo, New York : Created by Humans, an imprint of Rosen Publishing, 2027. | Series: The facts on famous artifacts | Includes glossary and index.
Identifiers: ISBN 9781534553194 (pbk.) | ISBN 9781534553200 (library bound) | ISBN 9781534553217 (ebook)
Subjects: LCSH: Parthenon (Athens, Greece)--Juvenile literature. | Athens (Greece)--Buildings, structures, etc.--Juvenile literature.
Classification: LCC NA281.H53 2027 | DDC 726.120809385--dc23

Manufactured in the United States of America

CPSIA Compliance Information: Batch #CSCBH27. For Further Information contact Rosen Publishing at 1-800-237-9932.

CONTENTS

STILL STANDING

The Parthenon is a temple in Athens, Greece, that was completed in 432 BCE. It rests atop the Acropolis, a **citadel** constructed on a raised area in the middle of the city. The Parthenon was built to honor the Greek goddess Athena. This ancient temple has been through numerous wars, yet still it stands!

You might be surprised to hear that many of the statues originally placed in the Parthenon centuries ago are now displayed in European museums. How did they get there? Why were they transported thousands of miles away from Athens? Read on to find out the whole story!

ARTI-FACT!

An artifact is something made by a human being, especially one of cultural or historical importance.

The Acropolis of Athens and its temple to Athena are one of the most noticeable sights in the world. They were made by human hands and minds!

ANCIENT GREECE

In the 8th century BCE, groups began to create **sovereign** communities around Greece called city-states. Some became very large—Sparta grew to about 300 square miles (780 sq km). Others were home to only about 100 people. These communities built city walls for protection from enemies.

ARTI-FACT!

Athens was named for its patron goddess, Athena. Greek mythology says that Athena was born, fully armored, from her father Zeus's forehead. She was the goddess of wisdom, warfare, handicrafts, law and justice, and more.

In 1897, architect William Crawford Smith designed and built a full-scale **replica** of the original Parthenon near Nashville, Tennessee. It's a museum today.

Many city-states were led by tyrants. In time, a fairer type of government began to form in city-states like Athens. Ancient Athens is considered the birthplace of Western **democracy**. It became a thriving center for art, theater, **technological** advancement, and philosophical discussion. Athens became a powerful and influential city-state in the 5th century BCE.

WHAT IS THE ACROPOLIS?

An acropolis is a fortified part of an ancient Greek city that was usually built on a hill overlooking the city. "Acro-" means high and "polis" means city. These areas had been used for many purposes over the centuries.

This 1846 painting by German artist Leo von Klenze is titled *The Acropolis at Athens*.

A Map of the Acropolis

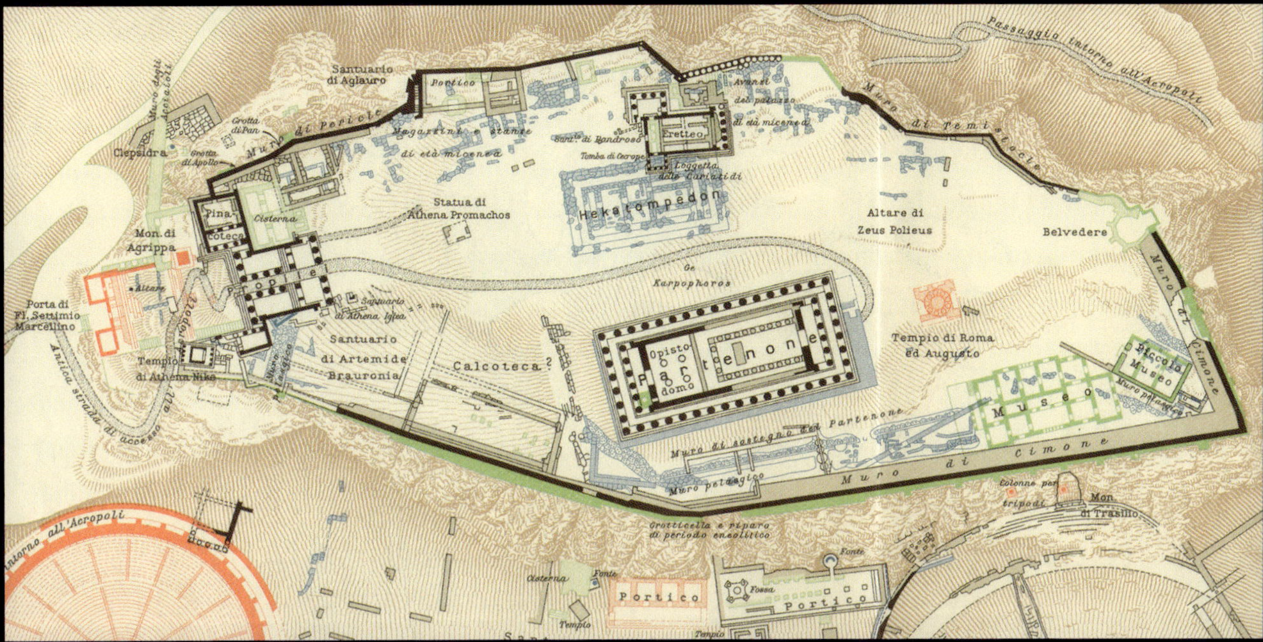

The Acropolis in Athens was first established by a group called the Mycenaeans in the 13th century BCE. They created buildings surrounded by a high wall to protect their ruler. Many temples, shrines, and other buildings were added over the years. It was a place long used for religious festivals. Many leaders fought for control of ancient Athens and the Acropolis over the years.

WAR WITH PERSIA

The Greco-Persian Wars (492–449 BCE) were fought between Greek city-states and Persia (now Iran). In 480 BEC, the Persian Empire attacked Athens and destroyed the Acropolis. This included a building historians call the "Older Parthenon."

Athens became the center of the Delian League, a collection of city-sates dedicated to protecting Greece from Persian forces. Athens became a military powerhouse during the Greco-Persian Wars. Their navy consisted mainly of small, fast ships called triremes. They were able to force a truce with the Persians, and the war came to an end in 449 BCE.

This piece of a carving made around 410 BCE is called the Lenormant Relief after the archaeologist who found it at the Acropolis in 1852. It shows a line of Athenian rowers powering a trireme.

The Athenian Trireme

Athenian triremes were high-tech naval ships for the time. They were about 120 feet (36.6 m) long and 18 feet (5.5 m) wide. Builders used light wood such as pine. Three rows of oars on each side of the ship were manned by 170 rowers. The front of the ship was covered in a metal called bronze so it could be used to ram other ships. Triremes had enough room to carry a pilot, several officers, and about 20 soldiers and archers.

BUILDING THE PARTHENON

In 447 BCE, the Athenian statesman and general Pericles started a program to rebuild the Parthenon to celebrate the end of the Greco-Persian Wars. Pericles hired the well-known Greek **architects** Ictinus and Callicrates, as well as the sculptor Phidias, to design the temple. The designers chose to build a Doric-style temple.

ARTI-FACT!

The Parthenon is often considered a high point in the use of the Doric building style. This style uses simple designs and features that are intended to show strength and **permanence**.

The Parthenon's Doric columns are fluted, meaning they have grooves that catch the light.

The Parthenon was dedicated to Athena in 438 BCE with the placement of a 37-foot (12 m) gold and ivory statue of the goddess. Decorative work and sculpting continued until 432 BCE. The temple's base is 23,000 square feet (2,137 sq m). Archaeologists think about 13,400 stones were used to create the temple.

Phidias created numerous marble statues of the Greek gods and goddesses for the Parthenon. The outside walls featured 92 carvings known as metopes. These showed ancient battles. Along the inside walls of the inner chamber ran a **frieze** decorated with bas-relief (raised) figures.

You might be surprised to learn that the Parthenon has very few straight lines or right angles! The builders did this on purpose. The columns are not perfectly straight—they bulge out in the middle. This makes them *look* perfectly straight to viewers. The temple's base is slightly dome-shaped so it doesn't look like it's sagging in the middle.

frieze from the Parthenon

The Parthenon was so well planned and constructed that viewers don't even notice the curves!

BACK TO WAR

Athens's success didn't last long. They became involved in the Peloponnesian War (431–404 BCE), which was mainly between Athens and Sparta. This resulted in a fall from power for Athens, as well as for democracy.

Over the centuries, the Parthenon was changed based on current events and politics. It was adapted to the use of the people in power. Some features were removed or updated. For example, Alexander the Great sent Persian shields to adorn the Parthenon after defeating the Persians in war. The shields were melted down long ago and the metal was reused for other projects.

This 1852 painting by German painter Phillip Foltz depicts Pericles making a speech during the Peloponnesian War. Behind him rises the Acropolis with the Parthenon at its center.

THE CHRISTIAN PARTHENON

Starting around 500 CE, Greece came under the power of the Eastern Roman Empire, also known as the Byzantine Empire. At first, Byzantine leaders left most of the Parthenon's outer walls alone. They converted the interior into a Christian church dedicated to Mary, the mother of Jesus. The giant statue of Athena had already been destroyed. In its place, Christian leaders built an altar and a stone throne.

ARTI-FACT!

The Byzantines made many structural changes to the interior of the Parthenon. They also cut away the surfaces of many of the metopes because they depicted imagery that offended the Christian faith.

For years, the Parthenon was an important place of pilgrimage for Christians. This means Christians were encouraged to visit and worship at the church sometime in their life.

During this time, the Parthenon was remade into a **basilica**. Later, it was named the Catholic Church of Athens. The area around the church was used as a cemetery for religious figures.

THE MUSLIM PARTHENON

The Parthenon was a Christian church for about 1,000 years. In 1458, the Ottoman Empire, also called the Turkish Empire, took Athens by force. Turkey was a Muslim country. They converted the Parthenon into a mosque, although they left many of the Christian artifacts where they found them.

A group of countries known as the Christian Holy **Alliance** threatened to attack the Ottomans in Athens. The Ottomans used the Parthenon for a storehouse of **ammunition**. An attack on Athens in 1687 caused the ammunition to explode. This resulted in many deaths and great destruction to the Parthenon.

This is a drawing of the battle that damaged the Parthenon in 1687.

Left in Ruins

The explosion in 1687 left the Parthenon in ruins. Many of the artifacts were looted, or stolen, and the grounds were **vandalized**. In the 1820s, Greek people fought for their independence from the Ottoman Empire. Ottoman forces removed hundreds of stone blocks from the Parthenon ruins. They also melted down iron clamps that had been used to keep blocks in place to make bullets. Very little of the original temple was left undamaged.

ART COLLECTOR OR STATUE STEALER?

In the early 1800s, the British ambassador to the Ottoman Empire, Lord Elgin, received approval from Ottoman rulers to study Grecian ruins. He was allowed to remove artifacts and send them to London, England. Between 1801 and 1805, Elgin oversaw the removal of about half the statues left in the ruins of the Parthenon.

Greece won its independence from the Ottoman Empire in 1832. Athens was selected as the capital for the new country. Most of the structures on the Acropolis that were built after the Roman Empire era were removed in an effort to return the area to its classical past.

British Parliament investigated Lord Elgin in 1816 and found his actions legal, and the "Elgin Marbles" became a permanent display in the British Museum of Art. However, the Greek government has never agreed with this decision.

Who Was Lord Elgin?

Thomas Bruce (1766–1841), the seventh earl of Elgin, was a British diplomat and art collector. He became ambassador to the Ottoman Empire in 1799. When Elgin arrived back in England in 1806, he found that many people, including the famous poet Lord Byron, did not approve of his actions. He was called a vandal and thief of ancient artifacts. For the rest of his life, Lord Elgin maintained that he was protecting the priceless artifacts from damage.

THE STATUE DISPUTE

The Greek government has been calling for the return of the Elgin Mables since they reclaimed control of their country. In 1983, they made a formal request to the British Museum for their permanent return to the Parthenon.

The British Museum Act of 1963 prevents the removal of any objects from the British Museum's collections. The British government has declined to change this law. Instead, they have offered to loan the statues to Greece on a limited basis. The dispute has led to difficulty between the two countries, and discussions are ongoing.

Outside of the United Kingdom, the Elgin Marbles are usually called the Parthenon Sculptures.

The Elgin Marbles

The Elgin Marbles collection has 17 statues, known as pediments, in various states of damage. They depict Greek gods and goddesses. The collection features 274 feet (83.5 m) of the frieze, which is about half of the total frieze. The collection also includes 15 metopes.

REBUILDING

Efforts to restore the Parthenon to its classical beauty increased in the 1970s. An archaeological committee called the Acropolis Restoration Project, led by Greek architect Maolis Korres, cataloged every artifact in the ruins of the Acropolis. They used computer technology to determine where each artifact was originally positioned. It was the world's largest jigsaw puzzle! This was just the start to a massive rebuilding project that continues to this day.

In 2009, the Acropolis Museum of Athens opened. Among its many artifacts, it houses statues from the Parthenon. It also has plaster copies of the statues currently on display in other museums.

ARTI-FACT!

UNESCO's World **Heritage** Convention has designated 1,248 sites as having important cultural or natural heritage, and that must be protected. In 1987, the Acropolis was added to this list of cherished locations.

In 2021, the committee of international peacekeepers UNESCO (United Nations Educational, Scientific and Cultural Organization) urged the United Kingdom government to work with the government of Greece to settle the long-lasting dispute.

WHAT DO YOU THINK?

The Parthenon has withstood a lot over the centuries—earthquakes, fires, wars, looting, vandalism, and explosions! Despite its long history and the many changes it has gone through, Greece has returned much of the building to its former, classical glory.

However, many people feel the Parthenon is incomplete due to the missing artifacts. The Greek government maintains that the approval Lord Elgin received from the Ottoman leaders is **invalid**, and that all artifacts taken from the site should be returned. The British Museum maintains that the artifacts have been kept safe and freely displayed to the public for years.

Where do you think the artifacts belong?

TIMELINE

13th century BCE	The Mycenaeans build the first Acropolis.
5th century BCE	The golden age of the ancient city-state of Athens
492–449 BCE	Greco-Roman Wars
480 BCE	Persian Empire destroys the Acropolis.
447 BCE	Pericles announces the rebuilding project.
431–404 BCE	Peloponnesian Wars
432 BCE	Construction is completed on the Parthenon.
500 CE	Byzantine Empire takes over Athens. The Parthenon becomes a Christian church.
1458	Ottoman Empire takes over Athens. The Parthenon becomes a Muslim mosque.
1687	The Christian Holy Alliance attacks Athens, causing a massive explosion.
1801–1805	Lord Elgin oversees the removal of artifacts from the Acropolis.
1816	The Elgin Marbles become a permanent display at the British Museum of Art.
1983	Greek government makes an official request for the return of the Elgin Marbles.
2021	UNESCO asks the British government to return the Elgin Marbles to Athens.

GLOSSARY

alliance: An association to further advance the interests of the members.
ammunition: Explosive objects used in war.
architect: A person who designs buildings and advises in their construction.
basilica: A Christian church with a dome and wide center aisle traditionally meant for community gatherings.
citadel: A fortress high above a city.
democracy: A government that gives individuals a voice in political choices.
frieze: A sculptured or ornamental band, especially around a building.
heritage: Something of value handed down from the past.
invalid: Having no force or effect. Not valid.
permanence: The state of being durable or long lasting.
replica: An exact copy of something.
sovereign: Politically independent.
technological: Having to do with technology, or the use of science in solving problems.
vandalize: To cause damage to property on purpose.

FOR MORE INFORMATION

BOOKS

DK staff. *Eyewitness Ancient Greece.* London, UK: DK Children, 2023

Kaiser, Brianna. *Athena, Goddess of War.* Minneapolis, MN: Lerner Publications, 2026.

WEBSITES

Acropolis Museum Kids
acropolismuseumkids.gr/en
The Acropolis Museum of Athens has an engaging and educational website especially for kids.

Ancient Greece: City of Sparta
www.ducksters.com/history/ancient_greece/sparta.php
Read all about the city-state of Sparta and find links to many related topics.

INDEX